THE NIGHT BEFORE
CHRISTMAS
IN TEXAS, THAT IS

By LEON A. HARRIS

Illustrated by

MEG WOHLBERG

PELICAN PUBLISHING COMPANY
GRETNA 1986

Copyright © 1952, 1980 by Leon A. Harris, Jr. ● All rights reserved ● Lithographed in the U.S.A. ● Printed in Japan
ISBN: 0-88289-175-8

'Twas the night before Christmas
In Texas, you know,
Way out on the prairie
(Without any snow).

Asleep in their cabin
Were Buddy and Sue,
A-dream' of Christmas,
Like me and like you.

Not stockings, but boots,
At the foot of their bed,
For this was in Texas,
What more need be said?

When all of a sudden
From out the still night,
There came such a ruckus
It gave me a fright!

And I saw 'cross the prairie
Like a shot from a gun,
A loaded-up buckboard
Come on at a run.

The driver was 'Geein',
And 'hawin', with a will.
The hosses (not reindeer)
He drove with such skill.

"Come on there, Buck, Pancho,
And Prince, to the right!
There'll be plenty of travelin'
For you-all tonight."

The driver in Levi's
And shirt that was red,
Had a ten-gallon Stetson
On top of his head.

As he stepped from the buckboard
He was really a sight,
With his beard and moustaches
So curly and white.

As he burst in the cabin
The children awoke,
And both so astonished
That neither one spoke.

And he filled up their boots
With such presents galore

That neither could think
Of a single thing more.

When Buddy recovered
The use of his jaws,
He asked, in a whisper,
"Are you Santa Claus?"

"Am I the REAL Santa?
Well, what do you think?"
And he smiled as he gave
A mysterious wink.

Then he leapt in his buckboard,
And called back, in his drawl,
"To all children of TEXAS,
MERRY CHRISTMAS, you-all!"